She Plays Sports

She Competes in Track and Field

By Trudy Becker

level 2 little blue readers

www.littlebluehousebooks.com

Little Blue House is distributed by North Star Editions:
sales@northstareditions.com | 888-417-0195

Produced for Little Blue House by Red Line Editorial.

Photographs ©: Shutterstock Images, cover, 4, 10, 13, 17, 21, 24 (top left), 24 (top right), 24 (bottom left); iStockphoto, 7, 9, 15, 18, 23, 24 (bottom right)

Library of Congress Control Number: 2022910479

ISBN
978-1-64619-707-1 (hardcover)
978-1-64619-739-2 (paperback)
978-1-64619-799-6 (ebook pdf)
978-1-64619-771-2 (hosted ebook)

Printed in the United States of America
Mankato, MN
012023

About the Author

Trudy Becker lives in Minneapolis, Minnesota. She likes exploring new places and loves anything involving books.

Table of Contents

Getting Ready

I compete in track and field.

I love track meets.

I get ready to compete.

I need many things for a meet.

I wear a uniform.

My clothes are light so I can run fast.

uniform

I put on my
running shoes.
The shoes are light too.
That helps me
move quickly.

At the Track

Sometimes I run races.

I get set on the starting line
and wait for the signal.

Then I start to run.

I run as fast as I can.

I pass other runners.

I stay focused until the finish line.

I do relay races too.
My teammate runs first,
then hands me the baton.
I take it and sprint around
the track.

baton

Sometimes I do hurdles.
I jump over
them carefully.
Nothing can slow
me down.

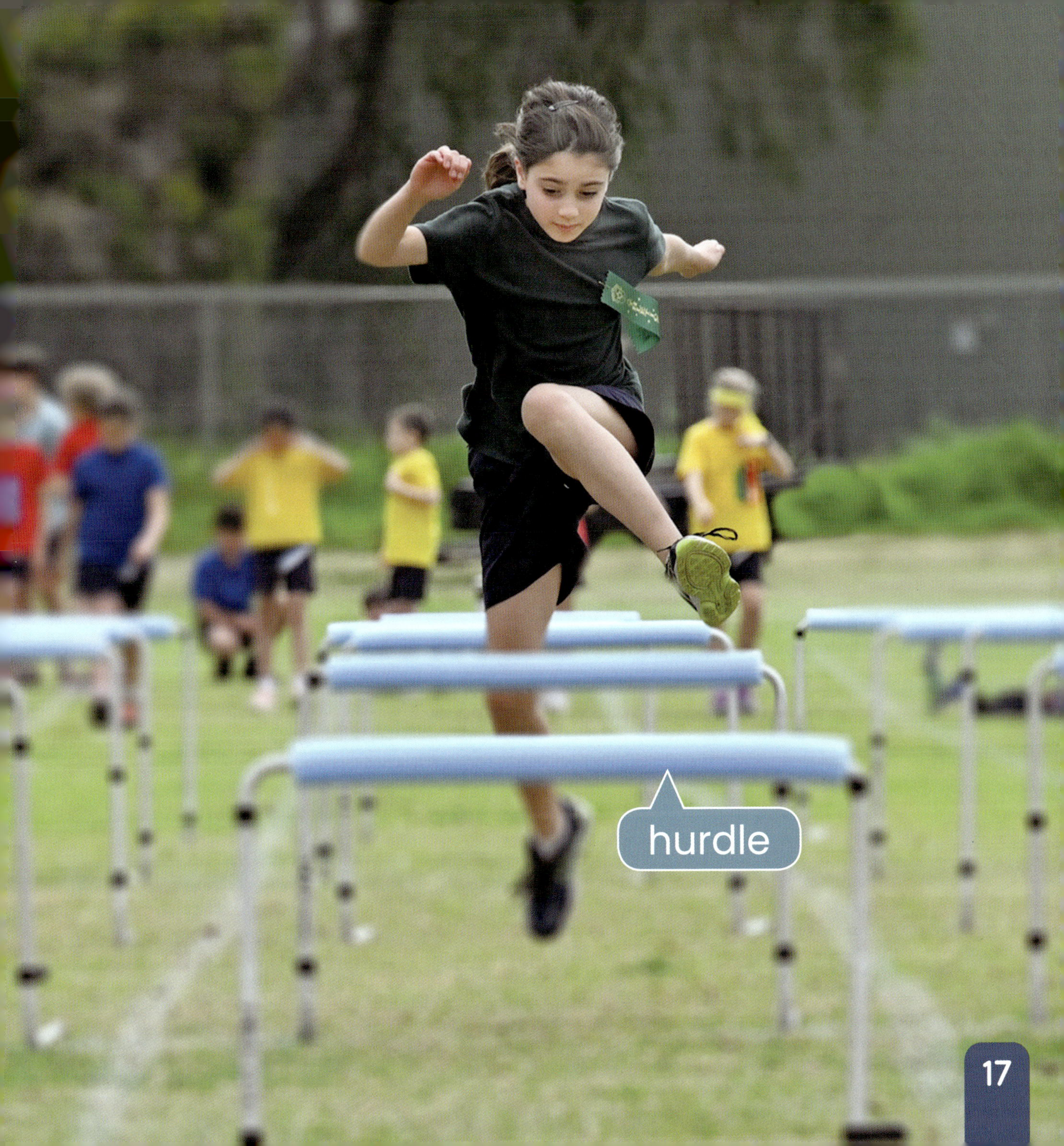
hurdle

shot

Field Events

I compete in field events too. One event is the shot put. I hold the shot by my neck. Then I turn my body and throw it.

Another event is the long jump.

I run to gain speed, then jump at the right time.

I leap into the pit.

I try to make it far.

pit

I also do the high jump.
I run, then throw my body
into the air.
I make it over the bar!
I love track and field.

bar

Glossary

baton

long jump

hurdles

shot put

Index